TRUST*Worthy*
STUDY GUIDE

Copyright © 2022 by Charla Turner

Published by AVAIL

All rights reserved. No portion of this book may be reproduced, stored in a retrieval system, or transmitted in any form or by any means—electronic, mechanical, photocopy, recording, scanning, or other—except for brief quotations in critical reviews or articles, without prior written permission of the author.

Scripture quotations marked KJV are taken from the King James Version of the Bible. Public domain. | Scripture quotations marked NIV are taken from the Holy Bible, New International Version®, NIV®. Copyright © 1973, 1978, 1984, 2011 by Biblica, Inc.™ Used by permission of Zondervan. All rights reserved worldwide. www.zondervan.com. The "NIV" and "New International Version" are trademarks registered in the United States Patent and Trademark Office by Biblica, Inc.™ | Scripture quotations marked NKJV are taken from the New King James Version®. Copyright © 1982 by Thomas Nelson. Used by permission. All rights reserved. | Scripture quotations marked NLT are taken from the Holy Bible, New Living Translation, copyright © 1996, 2004, 2015 by Tyndale House Foundation. Used by permission of Tyndale House Publishers, Inc., Carol Stream, Illinois 60188. All rights reserved. | Scripture quotations marked MSG are taken from THE MESSAGE, copyright © 1993, 1994, 1995, 1996, 2000, 2001, 2002 by Eugene H. Peterson. Used by permission of NavPress. All rights reserved. Represented by Tyndale House Publishers, Inc. | Scripture quotations marked ESV are from The ESV® Bible (The Holy Bible, English Standard Version®), copyright © 2001 by Crossway, a publishing ministry of Good News Publishers. Used by permission. All rights reserved. | Scripture quotations marked TPT are from The Passion Translation®. Copyright © 2017, 2018 by Passion & Fire Ministries, Inc. Used by permission. All rights reserved. ThePassionTranslation.com. |Scripture quotations marked NASB have been taken from the (NASB®) New American Standard Bible®, Copyright © 2020 by The Lockman Foundation. Used by permission. All rights reserved. www.lockman.org | Scripture quotations marked BSB are from The Holy Bible, Berean Study Bible, BSB, Copyright ©2016, 2020 by Bible Hub Used by Permission. All Rights Reserved Worldwide. | Scripture quotations marked TLV are taken from the Holy Scriptures, Tree of Life Version*. Copyright © 2014,2016 by the Tree of Life Bible Society. Used by permission of the Tree of Life Bible Society.

For foreign and subsidiary rights, contact the author.

Cover design: Sara Young

Cover Photo: Andrew van Tilborgh

ISBN: 978-1-957369-39-6   1 2 3 4 5 6 7 8 9 10

Printed in the United States of America

STUDY GUIDE

TRUST *Worthy*

How to deepen the
relationships you
need and avoid the
ones you don't.

CHARLA TURNER

AVAIL

CONTENTS

Introduction: When Trust Goes Wrong 6

Chapter 1. The Origin Of Trust Issues: Where Did It All Go Wrong? 12

Chapter 2. What Is Trust, And Why Is It So Important? 18

Chapter 3. Whom Should I Trust? A Tale of Two Voices: Which One Do I Trust Most? 24

Chapter 4. The Scent of Trust 30

Chapter 5. What's My Filter? 36

Chapter 6. When To Stop, Yield or Procees (Red, Yellow and Green Lights) 42

Chapter 7. Trust Principles 48

Chapter 8. Keeping Your Heart Safe 54

Chapter 9. Trusting God Through Hard Times 60

Chapter 10. Moving Forward After Betrayal and Trusting Again 66

Chapter 11. Relationship Philosophy 72

Epilogue: Safe Space, Safe People 78

INTRODUCTION

WHEN TRUST GOES WRONG

How can we know whom to trust, why we trust, what trust does, when to trust, how to heal from betrayal, and how to trust again?

READING TIME

As you read the Introduction: "When Trust Goes Wrong," in *TrustWorthy*, review, reflect on, and respond to the text by answering the following questions.

REFLECT AND TAKE ACTION:

In what situation have you wished desperately that God or someone with spiritual authority would just "tell" you what to do?

_____
_____
_____
_____

What conflicting thoughts ran through your head, preventing you from independently making what otherwise would seem a logical decision during that time?

_____
_____
_____
_____

How did you finally arrive at the answer that led to your decision?

_____
_____
_____
_____

What was the result?

_____
_____
_____
_____

To whom or what have you seen people go for answers to their life's questions?

Why might people seek assurance or guidance from those sources?

How effective are those means of direction?

> **REFLECT ON**
>
> *"I will instruct you and teach you in the way you should go;*
> *I will counsel you with my loving eye on you.*
> *Do not be like the horse or the mule,*
> *which have no understanding*
> *but must be controlled by bit and bridle*
> *or they will not come to you."*
>
> —Psalm 32:8-10 (NIV)

Consider the scripture above and answer the following questions:

How does God instruct and teach His people the way they should go?

_____
_____
_____
_____
_____
_____
_____

What might cause a person to resist His leading?

_____
_____
_____
_____
_____
_____
_____

How does God correct those who resist like horses and mules which require bits and bridles to be controlled?

_____
_____
_____
_____
_____
_____
_____

CHAPTER 1

THE ORIGIN OF TRUST ISSUES: WHERE DID IT ALL GO WRONG?

Trust goes wrong when we believe the thoughts of the created over the Creator.

READING TIME

As you read Chapter 1: "The Origin of Trust Issues: Where Did It All Go Wrong?" in *TrustWorthy*, review, reflect on, and respond to the text by answering the following questions.

REFLECT AND TAKE ACTION:

Is your natural inclination to be quick to trust with no reservations, or do you hold suspicion close and cynicism even closer?

_____
_____
_____
_____

How did the way you grew up impact your ability to trust? Consider those who cared for you as a child, where you lived and other events or circumstances that impacted you.

_____
_____
_____
_____
_____
_____

When have you overlooked or ignored the "red flags" because you felt you "needed" a relationship?

_____
_____
_____
_____
_____

Look back. When did you recognize that things were starting to go wrong? What lie was the enemy telling your betrayer or you?

_____
_____
_____
_____

Describe a time when a relationship brought you suffering. How much of it was because you were disconnected from God's goodness and connected to the enemy's lies

_____
_____
_____
_____

How firm is your conviction that God really does want what is best for you and that it can bring you joy despite your unmet desires and unanswered questions?

_____
_____
_____
_____

When have you been tempted in the suffering-pleasure-holiness cycle to take a shortcut or not trust God with a particular situation?

_____
_____
_____

How have you overcome shame and learn from your past?

REFLECT ON

"A worthless person, a wicked man, goes about with crooked speech, winks with his eyes, signals with his feet, points with his finger, with perverted heart devises evil, continually sowing discord; therefore calamity will come upon him suddenly; in a moment he will be broken beyond healing."

—*Proverbs 6:12-15 (ESV)*

"Beloved, never avenge yourselves, but leave it to the wrath of God, for it is written, 'Vengeance is mine, I will repay, says the Lord.'"

—*Romans 12:19 (ESV)*

Consider the scripture above and answer the following questions:

How do the behaviors listed in the Proverbs verses—crooked speech, a winking eye, a perverted heart, etc.—manifest in real life?

___

What does it look like when calamity comes upon a "worthless" or "wicked" person? How could that calamity be interpreted as God's vengeance?

___

How would you encourage someone who feels like their betrayer is getting away with the discord they've sown and the lives they've tried to ruin?

_____
_____
_____
_____

CHAPTER 2

WHAT IS TRUST, AND WHY IS IT SO IMPORTANT?

Trust isn't just one entity; it has many ingredients.

READING TIME

As you read Chapter 2: "What Is Trust, and Why Is It So Important?" in *TrustWorthy*, review, reflect on, and respond to the text by answering the following questions.

REFLECT AND TAKE ACTION:

After looking at the definitions of "trust" on page 52 of *TrustWorthy*, how do you define it?

_____
_____
_____
_____
_____
_____
_____

What role does trust play in your relationships?

- in your family

_____
_____
_____
_____
_____

- with your friends

_____
_____
_____
_____
_____

- at work

_____
_____
_____
_____

- in the world

_____
_____
_____
_____

How does your trust in God—that He is all-knowing, all-powerful, and ever-present—influence your ability to trust in those areas?

_____
_____
_____
_____

On page 44 of *TrustWorthy*, Charla references Brené Brown's acronym BRAVING[1] which the popular researcher uses to describe the ingredients of trust: **B**oundaries, **R**eliability, **A**ccountability, **V**ault, **I**ntegrity, **N**onjudgment, and **G**enerosity.

Which of those traits do you feel you exhibit consistently?

_____
_____
_____
_____

---

[1] Brené Brown, "SuperSoul Sessions: The Anatomy of Trust," Brené Brown, 25 Oct. 2021, brenebrown.com/videos/anatomy-trust-video/.

Which do you need to focus on developing?

_____
_____
_____

How can you specifically strengthen your weaker traits?

_____
_____
_____

Whom can you enlist to help you? What makes this person a suitable helper, and what is your plan to recruit them to your trust-building team?

_____
_____
_____

REFLECT ON

Trust in the LORD with all your heart and lean not on your own understanding; in all your ways submit to him, and he will make your paths straight.

—Proverbs 3:5-6 (NIV)

Consider the scripture above and answer the following questions:

What does it look like when a person is trusting the Lord with all their heart?

_____
_____
_____
_____
_____
_____
_____
_____

How do these verses cause you to look inward at yourself and evaluate your level of trust in God as well as trust in yourself?

_____
_____
_____
_____
_____
_____
_____

Charla says that God "defines our value and worth, and when we know our true identity is from Him, we can walk in confidence." How does this position us, so God can make our paths straight?

_____

_____

_____

_____

_____

_____

CHAPTER 3

WHOM SHOULD I TRUST? A TALE OF TWO VOICES: WHICH ONE DO I TRUST MOST?

It is imperative that we make sure we evaluate our inner dialogue and are careful to choose what voices we continue to listen to, align with, and ultimately trust.

READING TIME

As you read Chapter 3: "Whom Should I Trust? A Tale of Two Voices: Which One Do I Trust Most?" in *TrustWorthy*, review, reflect on, and respond to the text by answering the following questions.

REFLECT AND TAKE ACTION:

Which "voices" clamor for your attention most insistently right now? Where are they coming from?

_____
_____
_____
_____
_____
_____

What are the motivations behind their words?

_____
_____
_____
_____
_____
_____

What efforts do you make to hear God's voice?

_____
_____
_____
_____
_____
_____

How have you learned over time to distinguish God's voice from the enemy's?

_____
_____
_____
_____

Describe a time when you knew the enemy was trying to get you to believe one of his lies?

_____
_____
_____
_____

How did you handle that?

_____
_____
_____
_____

Read the following scriptures out loud, and meditate on them throughout the week. What practices can you apply when you know the enemy is trying to plant a lie in your mind?

- John 10:5 (NIV): "But they will never follow a stranger; in fact, they will run away from him because they do not recognize a stranger's voice."

_____
_____
_____
_____

- John 10:27 (ESV): "My sheep hear my voice, and I know them, and they follow me."

- Jeremiah 33:3 (ESV): "Call to me and I will answer you, and will tell you great and hidden things that you have not known."

- Jeremiah 29:13 (NIV): "You will seek me and find me when you seek me with all your heart."

- Isaiah 55:6 (ESV): "Seek the LORD while he may be found; call upon him while he is near."

- John 16:13 (BSB): "However, when the Spirit of truth comes, he will guide you into all truth. For He will not speak on His own, but He will speak what He hears, and He will declare to you what is to come."

REFLECT ON

"The good person out of the good treasure of his heart produces good, and the evil person out of his evil treasure produces evil, for out of the abundance of the heart his mouth speaks."

—*Luke 6:45 (ESV)*

Consider the scripture above and answer the following questions:

When have you seen Luke 6:45 to be true?

_____
_____
_____
_____

What do your words say about your belief system?

_____
_____
_____
_____
_____

How much of your inner dialogue is the result of how the significant people in your life talked to you when you were younger? Explain.

_____
_____
_____
_____

CHAPTER 4

THE SCENT OF TRUST

The experiences we have with those we trust or trusted cause us to decide whom we will trust in the future. It's as though each human interaction shapes and molds our trust capacity.

READING TIME

As you read Chapter 4: "The Scent of Trust" in *TrustWorthy*, review, reflect on, and respond to the text by answering the following questions.

REFLECT AND TAKE ACTION:

What associations do you make between certain scents and memories?

_____
_____
_____
_____
_____
_____

Which evoke a positive emotional response? How or what do they make you feel?

_____
_____
_____
_____
_____
_____

Which evoke a negative emotional or even physical response? How or what do they make you feel?

_____
_____
_____
_____
_____
_____

How well can you "sense" if a person is trustworthy or not?

___

When has trust proven to be a "tricky gift" for you?

___

What characteristics of a person—physical, verbal or behavioral—make you think someone is or is not trustworthy?

___

How likely are you to "listen to your gut" when it comes to determining whom to trust—or not? Why?

___

How can your gut and the Holy Spirit work together?

_____
_____
_____
_____

How can we use all the senses afforded to us to discern, develop, and deepen our relationships?

_____
_____
_____
_____

REFLECT ON

But thanks be to God, who always leads us as captives in Christ's triumphal procession and uses us to spread the aroma of the knowledge of him everywhere. For we are to God the pleasing aroma of Christ among those who are being saved and those who are perishing. To the one we are an aroma that brings death; to the other, an aroma that brings life. And who is equal to such a task?

—2 Corinthians 2:14-16 (NIV)

Consider the scripture above and answer the following questions:

What do you think the "aroma of the knowledge" or "the pleasing aroma" of Christ smells like?

_____
_____
_____
_____
_____
_____

In what ways is the aroma of Christ pleasing and life-giving to those who are being saved?

_____
_____
_____
_____
_____
_____

In what ways does it bring death to those who are perishing?

_____
_____
_____
_____

CHAPTER 5

WHAT'S MY FILTER?

From my perspective, most of the people really did want to help people and not hurt them. My world was a bit of a bubble: a squeaky-clean, fresh-smelling, light-and-airy, free-to-float, happy-song-singing bubble.

READING TIME

As you read Chapter 5: "What's My Filter" in *TrustWorthy*, review, reflect on, and respond to the text by answering the following questions.

REFLECT AND TAKE ACTION:

What is your trust philosophy?

_____
_____
_____
_____
_____
_____

How has that worked for you?

_____
_____
_____
_____
_____
_____
_____

Does your belief system give evidence of a "fixed" mindset or a "growth" mindset? On what do you base your assessment?

_____
_____
_____
_____
_____
_____

What fixed-mindset core beliefs do you need to get to the bottom of, so you can turn them into growth-mindset core beliefs?

___

Fill in the blank: The people that I trust tend to have the characteristics of:

___

How does each filter impact your ability to trust others and be trustworthy yourself?

- Belief System _____
  _____
  _____
  _____

- Wisdom and Knowledge _____
  _____
  _____
  _____

- Actions _____
  _____
  _____
  _____

- Personality_____
  _____
  _____
  _____

How can you check, evaluate, and adjust your belief system to make sure you are believing truth?

_____
_____
_____

Who can help you? What's your plan to enlist that person's help?

_____
_____
_____

REFLECT ON

Do not be conformed to this world, but be transformed by the renewal of your mind, that by testing you may discern what is the will of God, what is good and acceptable and perfect.

— *Romans 12:2 (ESV)*

Consider the scripture above and answer the following questions:

In what ways do you struggle with conforming to this world?

_____
_____
_____
_____
_____
_____
_____
_____
_____

What does "renewal of your mind" mean?

_____
_____
_____
_____
_____
_____
_____

How can people renew their minds, so they can discern the will of God?

_____
_____
_____
_____
_____
_____
_____
_____

CHAPTER 6

WHEN TO STOP, YIELD OR PROCEES (RED, YELLOW AND GREEN LIGHTS)

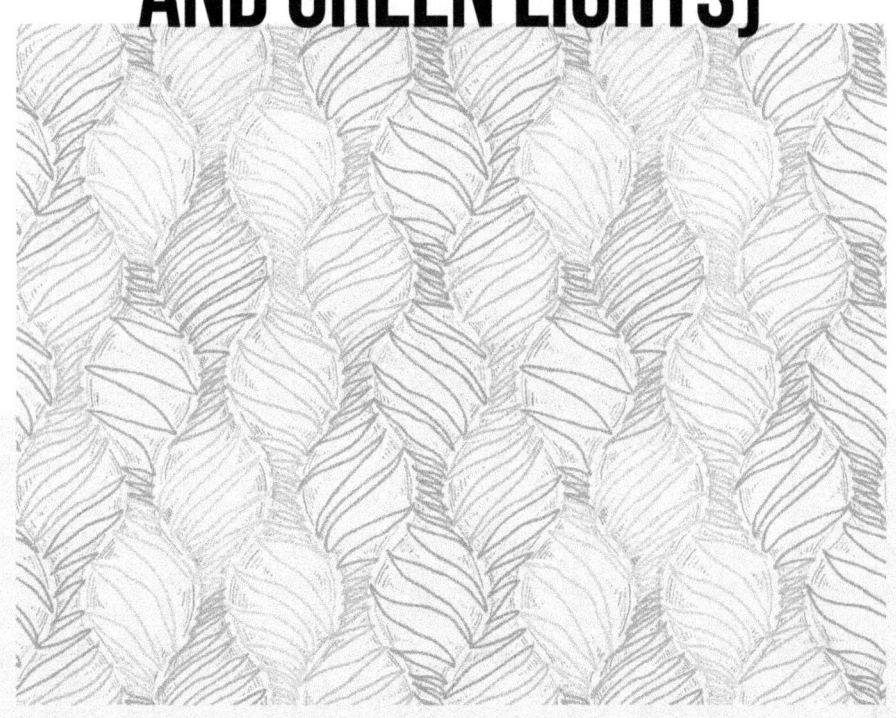

Regarding a person's red light: you can recognize it, be aware of it, pray for them, give them godly counsel and ask them to get the help they need, but you may want to discontinue forming a close relationship with a person who demonstrates any of red-light behaviors consistently.

READING TIME

As you read Chapter 6: "When to Stop, Yield, or Proceed (Red, Yellow, and Green Lights)" in *TrustWorthy*, review, reflect on, and respond to the text by answering the following questions.

REFLECT AND TAKE ACTION:

How do the unhealed areas of your life and your weaknesses hurt others or cause you to be hurt?

_____
_____
_____
_____
_____
_____

What parts of your personality have proven to be endearing to others? Which parts are repellant?

_____
_____
_____
_____
_____
_____
_____

Who have you found who is tough enough to withstand your quills?

_____
_____
_____
_____
_____
_____
_____

Whom have you had to walk away from because their quills were too sharp, or you didn't like the fruit you were seeing early on?

_____
_____
_____
_____
_____

What stood out most to you among the red, yellow, and green light behaviors?

_____
_____
_____
_____
_____

Which of your relationships are making you sharper or weaker? Give specific examples.

_____
_____
_____
_____

When have you found yourself in a toxic relationship? What characteristics were present? What did you do?

_____
_____
_____
_____

What areas of your life do you need to improve in relationally? What toxic characteristics do you struggle with?

_____
_____
_____
_____

What can you do today to be better in your relationships?

_____
_____
_____
_____

REFLECT ON

Brothers, if anyone is caught in any transgression, you who are spiritual should restore him in a spirit of gentleness. Keep watch on yourself, lest you too be tempted. Bear one another's burdens, and so fulfill the law of Christ.

—*Galatians 6:1-2 (ESV)*

Consider the scripture above and answer the following questions:

When have you borne another person's burden?

_____
_____
_____
_____
_____
_____
_____
_____

What did that look like, and what was the final result?

_____
_____
_____
_____
_____
_____
_____
_____

How did you judge whether the Lord was going to use you to restore that person gently or whether you should prevent the relationship from growing any deeper?

_____
_____
_____
_____
_____
_____
_____

CHAPTER 7

TRUST PRINCIPLES

*We are never obligated to stay in a relationship.
We are required to love and honor, but that doesn't
mean we have to be in relationship with them.*

READING TIME

As you read Chapter 7: "Trust Principles" in *TrustWorthy*, review, reflect on, and respond to the text by answering the following questions.

REFLECT AND TAKE ACTION:

When has the same person shown him or herself worthy of your trust in one situation but unworthy in another situation?

_____
_____
_____
_____
_____

If you had asked yourself, Who does this stand to benefit most? How might the situation have ended differently?

_____
_____
_____
_____
_____

How do you know if you should enter or stay in a relationship with someone whose trust rating is questionable, erratic or just spotty?

_____
_____
_____
_____
_____

When have you been so close to a relationship situation that you couldn't see the red flags? How might being part of and considering the perspectives of others in healthy community prevent that from happening?

_____
_____
_____
_____

Why do you think it is difficult for people to be vulnerable and admit fault in their relationships? What can you do to protect yourself from them?

_____
_____
_____
_____

Which trust "Rule of Thumb" listed on page 136 do you identify with the most? How can you stay safe by keeping it in mind?

_____
_____
_____
_____

Charla relates trust to currency. You can invest it, spend it, lose it, or waste it. It takes time to build it—and to build it back once you've lost it. How do you see those aspects play out in the real world?

_____
_____
_____
_____

What have you learned about building your relationships on principles as opposed to personalities?

_____
_____
_____
_____

REFLECT ON

It is better to be a poor but wise youth than an old and foolish king who refuses all advice. Such a youth could rise from poverty and succeed. He might even become king, though he has been in prison.

—Ecclesiastes 4:13-14 (NLT)

Consider the scripture above and answer the following questions:

Why might a "king" or someone with experience refuse advice?

_____
_____
_____
_____
_____
_____
_____
_____

If the youth was born poor in his own kingdom, how might his experiences in the prison have enriched his mind?

_____
_____
_____
_____
_____
_____
_____
_____

How can people show wisdom in their relationships?

CHAPTER 8

KEEPING YOUR HEART SAFE

We must define what's most important to us in a God-centered relationship. Then, we commit to becoming the best version of ourselves for God.

READING TIME

As you read Chapter 8: "Keeping Your Heart Safe" in *TrustWorthy*, review, reflect on, and respond to the text by answering the following questions.

REFLECT AND TAKE ACTION:

How can you tell what is in your heart at any given moment?

_____
_____
_____
_____
_____

Think of what is pulling at your heartstrings right now. If a person's eyes and ears are the gateways to their heart, what have you seen or heard that acted as a conduit?

_____
_____
_____
_____
_____

Charla says, "You have probably heard the saying 'Garbage in, garbage out,' but the opposite is also true, 'Treasure in, treasure out!'" When have you seen this to be true—in yourself and others?

_____
_____
_____
_____
_____

Do you naturally hold on to unforgiveness and offense, or are you quick to forgive? Answer for yourself, and then check with another person to see if they agree with you.

_____
_____
_____
_____

On what internal and external factors do you base your identity? How does that affect how you treat others and let them treat you?

_____
_____
_____
_____

What is your initial reaction to the thought of having a DTR—Define the Relationship—talk? What is more daunting: having to define your values and expectations or communicating them to someone else?

_____
_____
_____
_____

What benefits do you see in having a careful, intentional conversation where you ask a friend, romantic interest, coworker, boss, etc., what they value and expect from you in a given situation?

_____
_____
_____
_____

When might having a DTR talk be beneficial—even for people who've known each other for a long time?

_____
_____
_____
_____

How could a DTR talk be conducted, so the parties involved feel their relationship is organic?

_____
_____
_____

REFLECT ON

For you formed my inward parts; you knitted me together in my mother's womb. I praise you, for I am fearfully and wonderfully made. Wonderful are your works; my soul knows it very well.

—Psalm 119:13-14 (ESV)

Consider the scripture above and answer the following questions:

Why do you think there is such a disconnect between what God's Word says about people and what many people believe about themselves?

_____
_____
_____
_____
_____
_____
_____

How could you combine Romans 10:17 (ESV): "So faith comes from hearing, and hearing through the word of God" and the verses above to encourage someone who struggles with their value?

_____
_____
_____
_____
_____
_____
_____

CHAPTER 9

TRUSTING GOD THROUGH HARD TIMES

Trusting God does not mean that the chapters of our lives will be free from suffering or pain. It does mean that God will ultimately make meaning out of them.

READING TIME

As you read Chapter 9: "Trusting God Through Hard Times" in *TrustWorthy*, review, reflect on, and respond to the text by answering the following questions.

REFLECT AND TAKE ACTION:

What does it mean to trust God?

How does that play out in your daily life?

Whom do you admire who trusted God through great hardship? What was so inspiring about this person's actions and attitudes?

Whom do you know who became disappointed with God because He didn't meet their expectations? What have been the results of that situation?

_____
_____
_____
_____
_____

When have people or God exceeded your expectations? What were your feelings, and how did you communicate them?

_____
_____
_____
_____
_____

When have you been painfully disappointed by people or God? How did you process your pain? To whom did you communicate your feelings?

_____
_____
_____
_____
_____

What do you do in hard seasons that brings you peace and joy?

_____
_____
_____
_____

How could you implement STAY as Charla describes on pages 174-175 of *TrustWorthy*?

_____

_____

_____

_____

_____

What scripture/promise from God's Word can you stand on and meditate on during a season of disappointment?

_____

_____

_____

_____

_____

> **REFLECT ON**
>
> *And after you have suffered a little while, the God of all grace, who has called you to His eternal glory in Christ, will Himself restore, confirm, strengthen, and establish you.*
>
> —1 Peter 5:10 (ESV)

Consider the scripture above and answer the following questions:

When has God restored your broken heart or spirit?

_____
_____
_____
_____
_____
_____
_____
_____

How did you keep the faith when it felt like you had suffered for longer than "a little while"?

_____
_____
_____
_____
_____
_____
_____
_____

In what ways did God confirm, strengthen, and establish you?

_____
_____
_____
_____
_____
_____
_____

CHAPTER 10

MOVING FORWARD AFTER BETRAYAL AND TRUSTING AGAIN

God speaks to us in various ways. . . . I mean, if God could speak through a donkey, then I believe He could speak through a country song and even through me.

READING TIME

As you read Chapter 10: "Moving Forward after Betrayal and Trusting Again" in *TrustWorthy*, review, reflect on, and respond to the text by answering the following questions.

REFLECT AND TAKE ACTION:

When have rules meant to keep your heart safe and protected felt like restrictions to keep you from having fun?

_____
_____
_____
_____
_____
_____
_____

How did you respond to those rules?

_____
_____
_____
_____
_____
_____
_____

What were the repercussions of your response?

_____
_____
_____
_____
_____
_____
_____

How has the way you viewed those rules when you were younger influenced how you communicate rules to those under your authority?

___

How have you seen the Lord speak to people? How does He speak to you?

___

When has the Lord opened your eyes and allowed you to see clearly a situation that previously had caused you much distress and confusion?

___

Whom can you talk to when trust is proving to be tricky, the good in a relationship is mixed with bad, and you're not sure how much negative to endure?

___

Why is it a good idea for a person or a couple to see a professional counselor if they have differing views on what constitutes abuse and neglect?

REFLECT ON

No temptation has seized you except what is common to man. And God is faithful; He will not let you be tempted beyond what you can bear. But when you are tempted, He will also provide an escape, so that you can stand up under it.

—*1 Corinthians 10:15 (BSB)*

Consider the scripture above and answer the following questions:

What temptations have seized you that are common to all people?

_____
_____
_____
_____
_____
_____
_____
_____

What does it mean that God will not let you be tempted beyond what you can bear?

_____
_____
_____
_____
_____
_____

What manners of escape does God provide for those being tempted?

_____
_____
_____
_____
_____
_____
_____

CHAPTER 11

RELATIONSHIP PHILOSOPHY

As we grow and learn, we want to live our lives with intentionality—by design and not default.

READING TIME

As you read Chapter 11: "Relationship Philosophy" in *TrustWorthy*, review, reflect on, and respond to the text by answering the following questions.

REFLECT AND TAKE ACTION:

What do you find the most challenging in the art of relationships?

_____
_____
_____
_____
_____
_____

How have you been intentional in the past as you've attempted to overcome your relationship challenges?

_____
_____
_____
_____
_____
_____

As you prepare to come up with a "Relationship Philosophy" of your own, what are your overall feelings: anticipation, dread, etc.? Why?

_____
_____
_____
_____
_____

Take inventory of your various roles and the relationships that come with them. Answer the following questions for each role, and allow them to guide you as you define your relationship philosophy:

- What kind of a _____ (insert role) am I?

- What kind of a _____ (insert role) do I want to be?

_____
_____
_____
_____
_____
_____
_____

After you've answered the rest of the relationship philosophy questions on page 201 of *TrustWorthy*, create some "I am" or "I will" statements to describe how you want to operate in your relationships.

Charla believes: "You don't attract what you want; you attract what you are." In your mind's eye, what does your best version of you look and act like?

What are you trusting God for as you focus on being the best version of yourself?

REFLECT ON

Yahweh is my strength and my wraparound shield. When I fully trust in you, help is on the way. I jump for joy and burst forth with ecstatic, passionate praise! I will sing songs of what you mean to me! You will be the inner strength of all your people, Yahweh, the mighty protector of all, and the saving strength for all your anointed ones. Save your people whom you love, and bless your chosen ones. Be our shepherd leading us forward, forever carrying us in your arms!

—Psalm 28:7-9 (TPT)

Consider the scripture above and answer the following questions:

In what ways do the psalmist's words reflect your feelings about God?

_____
_____
_____
_____
_____
_____
_____
_____

How do you communicate to God what He means to you?

_____
_____
_____

Ask Him to shepherd you and lead you forward as you endeavor to honor Him through your relationship philosophy.

EPILOGUE

SAFE SPACE, SAFE PEOPLE

Knowledge is what to do. Wisdom is how to do it.

READING TIME

As you read the Epilogue: "Safe Space, Safe People" in *TrustWorthy*, review, reflect on, and respond to the text by answering the following questions.

REFLECT AND TAKE ACTION:

Describe your idea of a "safe space."

_____
_____
_____
_____
_____
_____
_____
_____
_____
_____

What would it take for your "safe space" to become a reality?

_____
_____
_____
_____
_____
_____
_____
_____
_____
_____
_____

How can you learn to be quiet and let God defend you against the enemy?

_____
_____
_____
_____
_____
_____
_____

Why is it true that the best gift we can give to people is sometimes the gift of goodbye? How can you also offer that gift to yourself?

_____
_____
_____
_____
_____
_____
_____

What is your greatest takeaway from *TrustWorthy*?

_____
_____
_____
_____
_____
_____
_____

REFLECT ON

For now we see but a faint reflection of riddles and mysteries as though reflected in a mirror, but one day we will see face-to-face. My understanding is incomplete now, but one day I will understand everything, just as everything about me has been fully understood. Until then, there are three things that remain: faith, hope, and love—yet love surpasses them all. So above all else, let love be the beautiful prize for which you run.

—*1 Corinthians 13:12-13 (TPT)*

Consider the scripture above and answer the following questions:

While your understanding is still incomplete, what has the Holy Spirit revealed to you on your *TrustWorthy* journey?

_____
_____
_____
_____
_____

What hope do you find in knowing that you are fully understood by God?

_____
_____
_____
_____
_____
_____
_____

Ask the Holy Spirit to give you joy as you pursue the beautiful prize for which you are running: love.

_____
_____
_____
_____
_____
_____
_____

www.ingramcontent.com/pod-product-compliance
Lightning Source LLC
Chambersburg PA
CBHW062119080426
42734CB00012B/2924